First Day In College

कालिज में पहला दिन

by Tabassum Ashraf

लेखिका

तबस्सुम अशरफ

Text copyright © Tabassum Ashraf 1999
Illustrations: Polly McMillan
Book design and artwork: David Andrassy
Hindi translation: The Translation and Interpretation Service,
Manchester City Council
Back cover photograph: R K Puri
Editor: Mohini Puri

Published and distributed by Gatehouse Books Ltd.,
Hulme Adult Education Centre, Stretford Road, Manchester M15 5FQ

Printed by RAP Ltd., Rochdale.

ISBN 0906 253 77 2

British Library cataloguing in publication data:
A catalogue record for this book is available from the British Library

Many thanks to Michaela Salmon, tutor at Plymouth Grove Adult Education
Centre, for encouraging her ESOL students to write, and contributing to the
selection process.

Many thanks also to piloting groups composed of ESOL students organised by
Nan Jackson, Co-ordinator of the Partnership Education Project at Rochdale
and Lyn Carter, ESOL Team Leader at Huddersfield Technical College.

Gatehouse is grateful for continued financial support from Manchester City
Council and North West Arts Board, and for financial assistance for the
development of the Asian Women's Writing and Publishing Project, from the
National Lottery Charities Board, Barrow-Cadbury Trust, Save and Prosper
Educational Trust, Kellogg's and Garfield Weston Foundation.

Our thanks for their ongoing support to Manchester Lifelong Learning.

Gatehouse is a member of The Federation of Worker Writers
& Community Publishers
Gatehouse Publishing Charity is a charity registered in England no. 1011042

Gatehouse provides an opportunity for writers to express their thoughts and
feelings on aspects of their lives.
The views expressed are not necessarily those of Gatehouse.

Dedication

This book is dedicated to the memory of
Sandra Softly who passed away
in December 1998.
Her contribution to the Asian Women's Project
was very much valued.

Introduction

From a very young age
I have always been interested in tasty food
and cooking a variety of dishes.
Trying out new recipes is my hobby.
I teach cookery at Chorlton workshop.
The students are ESOL* learners
and they learn English through cookery.
Reading and writing are also of interest to me.
These joyful pastimes have been with me
from school age.
At school and college
we often wrote stories and autobiographies.
My first college day
was a day of special remembrance.
Have a guess what happened on that day.
As you read on you will find out.
I trust you will enjoy this little effort of mine.
You will discover how we became fooled.
A special thank you goes to my husband
for his support and encouragement.
I would also like to thank Mohini Puri
for her valuable suggestions.
This book is dedicated to my three lovely children
Iqra, Saqib, and Azka.

Tabassum Ashraf.

*English For Speakers of Other Languages

परिचय

बहुत छोटी उमर से
मुझे हमेशा विभिन्न प्रकार के भोजन पकाने और
स्वादिष्ट भोजन में बहुत रूची रही है।
नये-नये पकवान बनाने की कोशिश करना मेरा प्रिय शौक है।
मैं चार्लटन वर्कशाप में भोजन कला सिखाती हूं।
वो इसौल (ESOL) विधार्थी हैं
और वो भोजन कला द्वारा अंग्रेज़ी सीखते हैं।
पढ़ना-लिखना भी मुझे बहुत प्रिय है।
समय बिताने की ये रूचियां मुझे
अपने स्कूल जीवन से ही प्रिय हैं।
स्कूल और कालिज के दौरान
हमने आमतौर पर कहानियां और आत्मकथाएं लिखी।
कालिज का मेरा पहला दिन
एक विशेष यादगार का दिन है।
ज़रा अंदाज़ा लगाये उस दिन क्या हुआ !
आप जैसे आगे पढ़ेंगें आपको पता चलेगा।
आशा है कि आपको मेरी इस छोटी सी कोशिश से बहुत आन्नद मिलेगा।
आपको पता चलेगा कि हम कैसे मूर्ख बन गई।
मैं अपने पति के सहयोग व प्रोत्साहन के लिये विशेष आभारी हूं।
मोहिनी पुरी का भी उनके उपयोगी सुझावों के लिये आभार प्रकट करती हूं।

समर्पण

यह पुस्तिका मेरे तीन प्यारे बच्चे
इकरा, साकिब और अज़का
के नाम समर्पित है

तबस्सुम अशरफ

I was seven
when I first saw somebody
go to college.
From then on I hoped and dreamed.
I dreamed that one day,
I too might be able to go to college.

1

मैं सात वर्ष की थी

जब मैंने पहली बार

किसी को कालिज जाते देखा

उस दिन से मेरे भीतर एक अभिलाषा व स्वप्न ने जन्म लिया

मैंने स्वप्न देखा कि एक दिन

मैं भी कालिज जा सकूंगी।

2

I had heard a lot about college life.
There you were free
to attend classes or not.
Weeks, months and years passed by.
At last, it was the end
of my school life.
I was sixteen.
I was so pleased
and my exams went very well.

मैंने कालिज जीवन के बारे में बहुत कुछ सुना हुआ था
वहां आपकी मर्जी पर होता है कि
आप अपनी क्लास में जायें या न जायें।
इस तरह हफ्ते, महीने और वर्षो गुज़र गये
आखिरकार, मेरे स्कूल जीवन का
अंत आ पहुंचा।
मैं सौलह वर्ष की थी
मैं बहुत खुश थी की मेरे
सारे पेपर बहुत अच्छे हुये थे।

It was now the summer holidays.
I began to look forward
to the end of the holiday.
I wanted my exam results.

अब गर्मियों की छुट्टियां चल रही थी
और मैं छुट्टियों के
समाप्त होने की प्रतीक्षा कर रही थी।
मुझे अपनी परीक्षा के परिणाम का इन्तज़ार था।

The results were published
in the local newspaper.
My father brought
a copy of the paper
home from his office.
When he got home,
the first thing he asked me
was my school roll number.

स्थानीय समाचार पत्र में
हमारे परिणाम प्रकाशित हुये।
मेरे पिताजी इसकी एक कापी
अपने ऑफिस से घर पर लाये।
जब वो घर पर आये,
तो सबसे पहले उन्होंने मेरे से
मेरे स्कूल का रोल नम्बर पूछा।

At first I was anxious,
worrying if I had failed or passed.
But, I pulled myself together
and told my father
my roll number.

पहले तो मैं बहुत उत्सुक थी,

चिंतिन्त हुई कि क्या मैं फ़ेल हूं या पास।

परन्तु मैने अपने आपको सम्भाला

और अपने पिताजी को अपना

रोल नम्बर बता दिया।

He discovered that
I had achieved first division!*
Everybody was so pleased for me.
We then had to decide
which college I would apply to.

*first division means getting marks over 70%

उन्होंने ढूंढ कर पता लगाया कि
मैने प्रथम श्रेणी में सफलता प्राप्त की है!
सभी मेरे लिये बहुत खुश थे।
तब हमें निर्णय करना पड़ा कि
मैं किस कालिज में अप्लाई करूं।

12

We were living in Multan at that time.
My Father would soon be posted
to another town.
Eventually, it was decided
that we would move to Khan Pur
where my grandparents lived.
The town had a degree college.

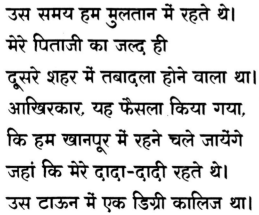

उस समय हम मुलतान में रहते थे।
मेरे पिताजी का जल्द ही
दूसरे शहर में तबादला होने वाला था।
आखिरकार, यह फैसला किया गया,
कि हम खानपूर में रहने चले जायेंगे
जहां कि मेरे दादा-दादी रहते थे।
उस टाऊन में एक डिग्री कालिज था।

14

After we had moved to Khan Pur,
I went with my father
and enrolled at the college.
At last, the holidays ended
and for the first time
I went to the college as a student.
I was so excited.

खानपूर में चले जाने के बाद,
मैं अपने पिताजी के साथ गई
और कालिज में दाख़िला ले लिया।
आख़िरकार, छुट्टियां समाप्त हुईं
और एक विधार्थी के नाते
मैं पहली बार कालिज में गई।
मैं बहुत उत्तेजित थी।

My dream was coming true.
Although I was happy,
I was afraid as well.
I had heard rumours
that the older students
played practical jokes
on new students.
My biggest worry was
that I had no friend there.

मेरा स्वप्न पूरा हो रहा था।

यद्यपि मैं बहुत प्रसन्न थी,

परन्तु मैं बहुत घबरा भी रही थी।

मैने अफवाहें सुनी हुई थी,

कि बड़े विधार्थी नये विधार्थीयों के साथ

बड़े मज़ाक करते हैं।

मेरी सबसे बड़ी चिन्ता यही थी

कि वहां मेरी कोई सहेली नही थी।

At last the big day came -
my first day at college.
All the students wore white
salwar kameez* and scarves.
The only difference in the uniform
from one year to the next
was the colour of the scarves.

*Salwar kameez is traditional Asian dress.
Salwar means trousers, kameez means top.

19

अंत में, जिस दिन का मुझे इंतज़ार था-
वो दिन आ गया-कालिज में मेरा पहला दिन।
सारे विधार्थीयों ने सफेद सलवार कमीज़
और चुन्नी पहनी हुई थी।
यूनिफार्म में केवल एक अन्तर था।
एक साल से दूसरे साल के विधार्थीयों के लिये
अलग-अलग रंग की चुन्नी थी।

All the new girls wore light pink scarves.
When I saw some girls
with pink scarves
I went to join them.
Second year girls wore blue scarves.
Senior girls in fourth year
wore white scarves.

सभी नई लड़कियों ने हल्के गुलाबी रंग की चुन्नी पहनी हुई थी।

जैसे ही मैंने गुलाबी रंग की

चुन्नी वाली लड़कियां देखी,

में उनके पास चली गई।

दूसरे वर्ष वाली लड़कियों ने नीली चुन्नी पहनी हुई थी।

चौथे वर्ष की सीनियर लड़कियों ने

सफेद चुन्नी पहनी हुई थी।

A girl with a white scarf
came over to us.
She said, "The lecturer
is calling you for assembly."
We followed her to the first year hall.
We asked if we could enter.

तभी सफेद रंग के स्कार्फ वाली

एक लड़की हमारे पास आई

उसने हमसे कहा, " लेक्चरार

आपको सभा के लिये बुला रही है"।

हम उसके पीछे-पीछे प्रथम वर्ष के हाल में गये।

हमने प्रवेश करने के लिये अनुमति मांगी।

The lecturer looked very young.
She also looked very angry.
She said, "Why are you late?
Didn't you know
where the assembly takes place?"
Of course, we first year girls kept quiet.
To think, we were getting into trouble
on our first day.

लेक्चरार उम्र की बहुत छोटी लग रही थी।

वो बहुत नाराज़ दिखाई देती थी।

उसने कहा, "आप देर से क्यों आई हो?

क्या आपको मालुम नहीं

कि सभा कहां होती है?"

यह सोच कर कि हम पहले दिन ही मुश्किल में फंस गई

हम प्रथम वर्ष की सभी लड़कियां चुप रहीं।

The lecturer asked each girl
to sing a song.
One or two of the girls sang out.
Some of us were very nervous.
At this point, an older lecturer
came into the room.
When the imposters saw
the real lecturer walk in,
they started chanting,
"First year fools, first year fools."
and they started laughing and clapping.

उस लेक्चरार ने प्रत्येक लड़की को

एक गाना गाने के लिये कहा।

एक या दो लड़कियों ने गाना गाया।

हम में से कुछ तो बहुत ज्यादा घबराई हुई थी।

उसी समय, एक बड़ी उम्र की

लेक्चरार ने कमरे में प्रवेश किया।

और जब नकली लेक्चरार ने

असली लेक्चरार को प्रवेश करते हुये देखा,

उन्होंने गाना गाना शुरू कर दिया,

"पहले साल के मूर्ख, पहले साल के मूर्ख"

और फिर वो हंसने और तालियां बजाने लग गई।

Well, the real lecturer was also amused
because these girls had tricked us.
Luckily, my turn to sing had not come.
I thought to myself,
"We who thought ourselves so clever,
have been fooled."
Whenever I look back
to that first day at college,
a smile appears on my face.

वास्तव में, असली लेक्चरार भी हंसने लग गई

क्योंकि इन लड़कियों ने हमको चकमा दे दिया था।

किस्मत से, अभी मेरी गाना गाने की बारी नहीं आई थी।

मैने सोचा,

"हम अपने आप को कितना हुशियार समझती थी,

और मूर्ख बन गई"

अब जब भी मैं अपने कालिज के,

पहले दिन की बात सोचती हूं,

तो मेरे चेहरे में मुस्कान खिल उठती है।

Gatehouse Books

Gatehouse is a unique publisher.

Our writers are adults who are developing their basic reading and writing skills. Their ideas and experiences make fascinating material for any reader, but are particularly relevant for adults working on their reading and writing skills. The writing strikes a chord – a shared experience of struggling against many odds.

The format of our books is clear and uncluttered. The language is familiar and the text is often line-broken, so that each line ends at a natural pause.

Gatehouse books are both popular and respected within Adult Basic Education throughout the English speaking world. They are also a valuable resource within secondary schools, Special Needs Education, Social Services and within the Prison Education Service and Probation Services.

Booklist available

Gatehouse Books
Hulme Adult Education Centre
Stretford Road
Manchester M15 5FQ
Tel/Fax: 0161 226 7152
E-mail: office@gatehousebooks.org.uk
Website: www.gatehousebooks.org.uk

The Gatehouse Publishing Charity is a registered charity reg. no. 1011042
Gatehouse Books Ltd., is a company limited by guarantee, reg. no. 2619614